Beautiful Birds

PEACOCKS

By Kristen Rajczak Nelson

Gareth Stevens
PUBLISHING

Please visit our website, www.garethstevens.com. For a free color catalog of all our high-quality books, call toll free 1-800-542-2595 or fax 1-877-542-2596.

Library of Congress Cataloging-in-Publication Data
Names: Rajczak Nelson, Kristen, author.
Title: Peacocks / Kristen Rajczak Nelson.
Description: New York : Gareth Stevens Publishing, [2023] | Series: Beautiful birds | Includes index.
Identifiers: LCCN 2021035985 (print) | LCCN 2021035986 (ebook) | ISBN 9781538275245 (set) | ISBN 9781538275252 (library binding) | ISBN 9781538275238 (paperback) | ISBN 9781538275269 (ebook)
Subjects: LCSH: Peafowl–Juvenile literature.
Classification: LCC QL696.G27 R35 2023 (print) | LCC QL696.G27 (ebook) | DDC 598.6/258–dc23
LC record available at https://lccn.loc.gov/2021035985
LC ebook record available at https://lccn.loc.gov/2021035986

First Edition

Published in 2023 by
Gareth Stevens Publishing
29 East 21st Street
New York, NY 10010

Editor: Kristen Nelson
Designer: Andrea Davison-Bartolotta

Photo credits: Cover Henk Bogaard/Shutterstock.com; p. 1 SAOWALAK SINGHAPAN/Shutterstock.com; p. 5 (top) SL-Photography/Shutterstock.com; p. 5 (bottom left) feathercollector/Shutterstock.com; p. 5 (bottom right) lessysebastian/Shutterstock.com; p. 7 tscreationz/Shutterstock.com; pp. 9, 24 (train) Naturali Images/Shutterstock.com; p. 11 Katarzyna Maksymiuk/Shutterstock.com; p. 13 Besides the Obvious/ Shutterstock.com; p. 15 Kalina-11/Shutterstock.com; p. 17 winistudios/Shutterstock.com; pp. 19, 24 (egg) veranija/Shutterstock.com; pp. 21, 24 (feather) Paskaran.T/Shutterstock.com; p. 23 Caius Gheorghe/ Shutterstock.com.

Printed in the United States of America

CPSIA compliance information: Batch #CSGS23: For further information contact Gareth Stevens, New York, New York at 1-800-542-2595.

Contents

Peacocks are birds.
There are three kinds.

One kind lives in India.

Males are colorful.
They have a long tail.
This is a train.

They lift their tail.
It looks like eyes!

They live in forests.

They eat bugs
and plants.
They eat small
animals too.

They gather in groups.
This is called a party.

Mothers lay eggs.

Babies come out
of eggs.
They are covered
in feathers!

They can fly at one week old.

Words to Know

egg

feather

train

Index